Alfred Henry Lewis

By Abe C. Ravitz

California State University,
Dominguez Hills

Editors: Wayne Chatterton
James H. Maguire

Business Manager:
James Hadden

Cover Design and Illustration
by Arny Skov, Copyright 1978

Boise State University, Boise, Idaho

Library of Congress Card No. 78-052560

International Standard Book No. 0-88430-056-0

Permission was granted to the author to quote from manuscript material in the collections of the Henry E. Huntington Library, San Marino, California.

Printed in the United States of America by
The Caxton Printers, Ltd.
Caldwell, Idaho

Alfred Henry Lewis

Alfred Henry Lewis

He was a cowboy and a lawyer, a journalist and a novelist. At ease passing the time of day with drifters in front of Melinda's House of Call at Watrous (Mora County) in the sparse territory of New Mexico or debating socio-economic philosophy with sophisticated Tammany politicians just outside City Hall in New York, Alfred Henry Lewis—Western regionalist and Eastern muckraker—was enchanted by America's land of legend and myth beyond the frontier, and he forever glanced backward with nostalgia at his "pampas years," when he roved "for many moons" between "the Canadian in the Panhandle and the Gila in Arizona." Although he eventually established himself as a big-city newspaperman associated as editorialist and Washington Bureau Chief with William Randolph Hearst—to whom Lewis dedicated his first published volume of Western sketches— the man's major orientation was not toward the "scoop," or other sensationalist copy for printer's ink. The glamour of his early experiences focussed Lewis's creative vision on territories beyond the Mississippi: Kansas City, Missouri; Las Vegas, New Mexico; Tombstone, Arizona. In at least seven books he closely described life in a frontier town as seen through the eyes of an elderly prairie dog called, simply, the Old Cattleman, whose dialect wisdom brought Old West perspectives into the mind's eye of Eastern readers. Indeed, according to historian Howard Mumford Jones, the famed raconteur of Alfred Henry Lewis soon became as legendary a figure hovering over the American landscape as "Captain John Smith and Daniel Boone" (*The*

Age of Energy: Varieties of American Experience, 1865-1915, p. 89).

By his own reckoning it was not until 1889 that Lewis turned his attention seriously to writing. He was thirty-two years old at the time, had just decided to move on from the habitat of "mule and steer, mesquite and cactus," and had come to Kansas City, then in the midst of a real estate boom. Quickly, Lewis bought, sold, speculated; he made money, spent it, and lost it. And when, inevitably, the land bubble burst and the need to earn a living began to press, he decided to try his hand at composition. The backgrounds he personally presented to Jack Nuckles, a city editor of the Kansas City *Times,* were clearly formidable. His potential, evolving from a life of diverse experience, was obviously worth tapping.

Born on January 20, 1857 (the date documented by Lewis's brother), in Cleveland, Ohio, the son of Isaac Jefferson and Harriet Tracy Lewis, Alfred Henry Lewis was educated in local schools; and manifesting no interest in following his father's trade of carpentry, he read law during those days of free and easy academic requirements, and was admitted to the Ohio bar in 1876. Successful as a lawyer, young Lewis by 1880 had risen to the position of City Prosecuting Attorney. But when his family picked up and moved westward, Lewis, feeling the itch of wanderlust, decided to give up his practice and accompany them.

At this point his movements across both the settled and uncharted American West become somewhat blurred and even spastic. But evidently, before his literary muse irresistibly beckoned, and while seeking to find himself, Lewis had logged much time in camp, on the range, and behind six-mule teams. The materials of this Western experience brought to his literary perception an awareness of the primitive frontier similar in emotional depth to the prairie discoveries made by illustrious Lewis contemporaries: painter Frederic Remington, novelist Emerson Hough, and plainsman-dilettante Theodore Roosevelt.

These celebrities developed stereotypical views of life along the borders of the virgin land, and their frontier stereotypes ultimately congealed to form the Alfred Henry Lewis Western strategy.

These commonly-held frontier viewpoints, accepted whole-heartedly in their day, are not pretty to contemporary Americans. "Jews, Injuns, Chinamen, Italians, Huns," wrote Remington to his friend Poultney Bigelow, May, 1893, in a letter now preserved in an issue of the *New York State Historical Association Quarterly*, "the rubbish of the Earth—I hate. I've got some Winchesters and when the massacring begins, I can get my share of 'em, and what's more, I will" (X, 1929, 46). Lending substance to these repulsive attitudes so prevalent on the teeming plains was popular novelist Emerson Hough, who in 1897 had detailed for his book *The Story of a Cowboy* this picture of social dynamics in the Western community: "The Jew did not come from Kansas, but dropped down from above, came up from below, or blew in upon the wind, no one knew how but he was always there. He advertised in the local paper, complaining about the rates, of course" (p. 241). Alongside such Know-Nothingism was included a belief in the essential inferiority of Indians and Mexicans, as well as adherence to Teddy Roosevelt's emphasis on the "strenuous life." Innocent, naive portraits of the hunter as gentleman were set alongside a superficial presentation of the West as a majestic spectacle—not as a chaotic region developing with severe growing pains. Such distorted views of reality helped establish in Alfred Henry Lewis the philosophical underpinnings that marked pseudonymous Dan Quin (only one "n" Lewis cautioned an editor in 1895), author of the Wolfville tales and "creator" of the Old Cattleman.

Yet there came to exist a unique literary interplay between the social and political realism in his Eastern fiction and the romantic and naturalistic tendencies of his Western prose. The tawdry back alleys and criminal hangouts populated by the vulgar underworld characters of New York's Mulberry Bend—the likes of Candy Phil, Indian Louie, Irish Wop, Nigger Mike, and Paper-Box Johnny—were classed in the Lewis imagination with his heroic figures, his giants in the West: "The cowboy is a youth of sober quiet dignity. There is a deal of deep politeness and nothing of epithet, insult or horseplay where everybody wears a gun. . . . On the range the cowboy is quiet, just and peaceable" (*Wolfville Nights,* pp. 10, 11). Fact and fancy, then, helped generate the conflict which produced the art of Alfred Henry Lewis.

Lewis had married Alice Ewing of Richfield, Ohio, and his pen had become their means of support. His interests in journalism and fiction were varied and wide. The whole time during which he was turning out successful yarns of sagebrush and tumbleweed, Lewis was deeply involved in local and national politics, covering crucial scenes of government activity on all levels and exercising his considerable press credentials. He came to be known as a steady reporter, proud of his newspaper connections and dedicated to the principles of a free press: "Now the newspapers . . . are the police of politics. It is their duty to keep posted concerning the plans and deeds of politicians, just as it is the duty of regular police to keep posted concerning the plans and deeds of burglars, or what others are at criminal warfare with the law," he soundly observed in his "Confessions of a Newspaper Man" (*Human Life,* June 1906, p. 7). So it was with great enthusiasm that Lewis journeyed to Washington in the early nineties to take a job placing him in the whirlpool of America's political influence and intrigue. With tongue in cheek he asserted his materialistic motivation for the hegira eastward: "When I shook the Western dust from my moccasins and started for Washington, I was looking for honor and money"; but he quickly went on to add that a search for honor alone would have kept him in the West (*Human Life*, May 1906, p. 7).

A frontier rugged individualist, yet an idealistic democrat, Lewis strongly advocated the belief that government accurately reflected the moral and ethical stance of the general electorate, no better, no worse. He had advised and encouraged his readers in the *Verdict*: "Be pure and your government will be pure; be brave and it will have courage; be free, and freedom will abide in your high places and descend therefrom to the rabble least among you. Be dogs and you will have a dog government—a kennel, a collar, a bone to gnaw and a chain to clank" (IV, November 12, 1900, p. 3). Still, because he worked in such close proximity to urban American society during these tumultuous years of reform and scandal, Lewis became cynical toward politics. Perhaps it was largely as an escape from that corrupt urban world that he created the mythical community of Wolfville, whose citizens found efficient, expedient solutions for even the most complex social dilemmas. Law was explicit. Justice was swift and sure. The alleged existence of Absolute Good and Evil simplified moral questions. With crude but effective Western analogies, Lewis once articulated his growing dissatisfaction with the ways in which Eastern society seemed to be evolving: "At that time I was a democrat; I have since become politically nothing, my disgust with democrats being exceeded only by my disgust of republicans. If I'd stayed away from Washington, I might have remained a democrat [but] my democracy began to hack for a corner, and pull a gun. It is still in the corner, still shooting . . . ." (*Human Life*, May 1906, p. 6).

And so it was that Alfred Henry Lewis—a man who had worked as a ranch hand for prominent citizens of Meade County, Kansas, a man who had driven cattle to Dodge City, who had wandered about the Texas Panhandle, and who had followed an adventurous trail into southeastern Arizona—became at length a career newsman and a successful free-lance writer specializing in political reportage and the American West. William Randolph Hearst's *Cosmopolitan* magazine was a frequent repository of the A. H. Lewis word; his versatile pen eventually gained for him the number one position in Hearst's significant Washington operation. The work schedule, to be sure, was ferocious. Writing to well-known editor and magazine manager Albert Bigelow Paine on August 30, 1895, Lewis described his daily routine: "I don't get down until about 4 in the evening. After that hour, and indeed until 5 the next morning, you will find me at my office in the [Washington] Post building" (MS., Henry E. Huntington Library). Congressional exposé, reform, and wire-service news were not Lewis's total concerns during those long hours, for the literary call of the West was close by his ear, and on October 11, 1895, he informed Paine about his progress on some Western tales: "I will write you later about the Old Cattleman stuff. It may be that until January when the Stokes people print my book [*Wolfville*] I cannot switch the stuff, but will have to invent another series of Western sketches for your special behoof" (MS., Huntington Library).

Lewis, indeed, maintained a grueling pace for the rest of his life. He edited and single-handedly wrote *The Verdict*, a Democratic sheet subsidized by Oliver Hazard Belmont Perry; and although it was a partisan political organ, Lewis managed to bootleg several *Wolfville Nights* sketches into the issues. He wrote on politics, on the problems of cities, even on so pretentious a topic as man's reason for being. *Human Life* in 1906 serialized Lewis's "Confessions of a Newspaper Man." This publication not only revealed his often provocative, challenging opinions of those who were euphemistically called "malefactors of great wealth," but it also helped illuminate some of Lewis's Western travels and the use he made of them in his art.

Lewis and his wife (they had no children) eventually moved to New York City, the center of the newspaper and publishing businesses. His life continued to be his writing, and while he prowled vice-ridden districts of lower Manhattan and furtively walked the streets of "Gangland" in the company of Detective Val O'Farrell seeking bizarre materials for his fiction, Lewis primarily concentrated on sharpening his recollections of those happy past times he had spent on the open plains. Though he was now surrounded by partisan newspaper writing in this very heyday of yellow journalism, his years back East were actually uneventful. Alfred Henry Lewis died on December 23, 1914. To the day of his death the man's youthful exposure to the American West had remained his paramount experience. While he developed great skill in reporting city life with the sharp eye of an aggressive, perceptive journalist, he mythologized the West with a conscious artist's dedication.

There was a frivolous as well as a serious aspect to the Eastern prose of Alfred Henry Lewis. On the one hand, during the early twentieth-century craze for historical novels in the American literary market place, he composed *Peggy O'Neal* (1902), an inconsequential period-piece that was set amidst the heady aroma of magnolias and honeysuckle in the ante-bellum South, when themes of Nullification and States Rights were superseded by unthinking patriotism and love. On the other hand, he published a well-researched, well-received political biography of Richard Croker, notorious Tammany boss, to complement the series of popular articles he had written for *Cosmopolitan* on "The Owners of America." These "owners" were men like Carnegie, Morgan, and Rockefeller "who are the real . . . rulers of the United States with various degrees of power in control of the industries" (June 1908, p. 3).

These Eastern writings of Lewis, furthermore, examine prevalent concerns that troubled American reformers and philanthropists as these writers surveyed the urban jungles: ghetto tenements swarming with disease, poverty, and vice. Side by side with the underworld cliques and cigar-chewing ward heelers

11

were those unfortunate victims of Bossism, of The Machine, and of the Law of Club and Fang which ruled supreme. In the ruthless scheme of evolutionary Social Darwinism brute strength was the mainspring of society. The force was epitomized by organized crime and its affiliated political corruption. Lewis described these conditions in *The Apaches of New York* (1912): "Gangland discusses things social, commercial, political, and freely forms and gives opinions. From a panic in Wall Street to the making of a President, nothing comes or goes uncommented upon and unticketed in Gangland" ("The Wages of the Snitch," p. 162). All the Apache tales, as a matter of fact, deal with crime and social decadence, stick-ups and safe-cracking, Tong Wars and house-breaking, gang rub-outs and opium smoking, confidence games and prostitution. Lewis's purpose was "to show you how the other half lives—in New York" (*Apaches*, p. 5).

In *Confessions of a Detective* (1906), Alfred Henry Lewis heatedly chastizes the collusion of law, politics, and citizen apathy:

> And when the last word is said, it's the public's fault. It permits the machine to pick out its mayor, and through him its police. It is the public who does this; and, when police things go wrong, the public shouldn't whine. Those who keep monkeys must pay for the glasses they break; that, too, whether the monkeys are kept in the City Hall or at Police Headquarters in Mulberry Street. (p. 81)

But in writing *The Boss* (1903)—subtitled *How He Came to Rule New York*—and in dedicating it to his friend George Horace Lorimer, publisher of the *Saturday Evening Post,* Lewis in a like manner revealed little sympathy for the *haut monde* that was Uptown Society:

> It is that circle where discussion concerns itself with

nothing more onerous than golf or paper-chases or single-stickers or polo or balls or scandals; where there is no literature save the literature of the bankbook; where snobs invent a pedigree and play at caste; where folks give lawn parties to dogs and dinners to which monkeys come as guests of honor; where quarrels occur over questions of precedence between a mosquito and a flea; where pleasure is a trade and idleness an occupation; in short, it is that place where the race, bruised of riches, has turned cancerous and begun to rot. (pp. 252-253)

On all levels, then, life in the city is dangerous and predatory; the Plutocracy reigns, and the Boss, whose muscle has enabled him to unify his control over law, politics, and the private citizens, never hesitates to flaunt or to use his power: "Let me tell you one thing . . . unless you walk with care and talk with care, you are no better than a lost man. One word, one look, and I'll snuff you out between my thumb and finger as I might a candle" (*Boss*, p. 270) .

Whether he was delineating Eastern life in sweatshops or drawing rooms, stuss-parlors ("stuss" was an Eastern version of faro) or fashionable clubs, Alfred Henry Lewis fixed a suspicious, contemptuous eye upon the city. Trying to mine his Washington experiences by writing a novel called *The President* (1904), he closely examined the processes of politics on a national scale, emphasizing pork barrel and bucket-shop intrigue. Lewis's version of his West, however, was never far from his mind, and he drew this analogy between politics and ephemerality:

Mayhap there be those among you who have "punched" the casual cow, and whose beef wanderings included the drear wide-stretching waste yclept the Texas Panhandle. If so you have noted, studded hither and yon

about the scene, certain conical hillocks or mountain-
ettes of sand. Those dwarf sand-mountains were born
of the labor of the winds, which in those distant regions
are famous for persistent, not to say pertinacious, industry. Given a right direction, the wind in its sand-drift-
ing will build you one of those sandcones almost while
you wait. The said cone will grow as a stocking grows
beneath the clicking needles of some ancient dame.
Again, the wind, reversing in the dance, will unravel
the sand-cone and carry it off to powder it about the
plain. The sand-cone will vanish in a night, as it came
in a night, and what was its site will be swept as flatly
clean as any threshing floor. (pp. 472-473)

Alfred Henry Lewis, then, was an Eastern reporter and an
interpreter of the urban scene. True, he mixed his realism
with some flimsy romanticist effects. The escape from the
ghetto was ever a throbbing hope for the prisoners immured
there. Even his abandoned girls yearned toward imaginary
princes who might come slumming through Great Jones
Street, who might notice Pretty Agnes, Molly Squint, or Goldie
Cora, and who might whisk the lucky one uptown to freedom.
These things never really happened, however, and Lewis never
suggested that they commonly did. Reality of motive and fidelity
of purpose were constant factors in his depiction of life along the
Five Points of New York. Love was always subservient to graft,
a ring on the finger never challenged a "gatt" in the pocket, the
opulent mansion never supplanted the tenement with its opium
fumes and its airshaft. Although he recognized the hopeless-
ness of the bottom-dogs, the alienated ones in the continuous
struggle with the intimidating forces of their lives, Lewis felt
deep sympathy for them in their plight. He thought there must
be ways to help alleviate the wholesale suffering he saw in his
wanderings as a reporter about the city. In a *Cosmopolitan* essay

published in October 1911, he tried to explain some of his own ambivalent feelings: "Those who think most clearly, reason most coldly, are not always the truest ones, and the heart is often wiser than the head" (p. 656). The American West presented Alfred Henry Lewis with the possibility of spiritual as well as literary fulfillment. The West offered him a chance to direct his vision toward what appeared to be a basic society that was free from the complications which modern civilization had inflicted upon the East.

The Western Community of Wolfville, modeled loosely after Tombstone, Arizona, came to be celebrated by Alfred Henry Lewis in seven popular volumes: *Wolfville* (1897), *Sandburrs* (1900), *Wolfville Days* (1902), *The Black Lion Inn* (1903), *Wolfville Nights* (1902), *Wolfville Folks* (1908), and *Faro Nell and Her Friends* (1913). It is a typical, rowdy frontier town where time is calculated by the drinking hour, where an active "vig'lance committee" maintains appropriate discipline and helps enforce the law, where Chinks (Chinese), Greasers (Mexicans), Injuns, and evangelists are treated with equal contempt, and where The Old Cattleman, a "grizzled raconteur," narrates tales of the town's past and present in the colorful argot of cowboy and gambler. Dan Quin is the alleged scribe who has recorded the fractured syntax of the Cattleman's freewheeling dialect; and to best fit the simple, uncomplicated structure of life in the "camp" of Wolfville, the story-telling "will be crude, abrupt, and meagre" (Preface, *Wolfville*).

Yet intermixed with anecdotes of sad consequence and narratives of primitive violence are moments reserved by The Old Cattleman and his cronies to deliver sententious observations upon the philosophy of human nature and its inexplicable vagaries: "Gamblers by nacher are romantic; a business gent roosts close to the ground. One is 'motional; the other's as hard an' pulseless as a iron wedge. The former's a bird, an' gaily spends his onthinkin' time among the clouds; the latter never

15

soars higher than he can lift himse'f on wings of bricks an' mortar" (*Wolfville Folks,* p. 24). Or from Doc Peets, "the best eddicated gent between the Colorado an' the Rio Grande," a wry assessment of the effete Eastern sensibility: "The big trouble with the East is it's not only ignorant, like I says, but ignorant in a pin-head way of se'f importance. It'll prance forth an' look the West over, towerist fashion, through the distortin' medium of a Pullman kyar window, an' go back bent double onder the idee it's got the Western picture from foretop to fetlock" (*Wolfville Folks,* p. 283).

Visited frequently by a variety of tenderfeet and shorthorns from the East, the stable parochial population of Wolfville reflects in attitude, deed, and word a Western ethos characterized by a detached sense of time—or timelessness—as transcendental as the ocean-like prairie. Furthermore, all life in the town is adorned by a bizarre mood of theatricality which equally pervades with Gothic overtones an innocuous game of faro at the Red Light or a quietly pedestrian meal at the O.K. House. There are, too, the common Western elements of escapist romance created by the suggestion of an imaginative flight back into a better place and time far away from oppressive, intimidating responsibilities inherent in modern urban life.

Lewis's Wolfville, though, did not evolve as a Western cowtown with characteristic local color, nor did it develop by stages of Lewis's artistic strategy into a complex microcosm, a self-contained land linked only to the outside world by the Tucson stage. Wolfville, rather, began and remained a fully-matured community, stable and unchanging throughout all of Lewis's Western regionalist productions. Therefore, the most advantageous manner of analyzing the man's work and the quality of life in his southeastern Arizona town is not chronological, but thematic. Seen thematically, the Lewis creative aesthetic and the Lewis literary vision of the American West emerge in their clearest confluence.

Fate controls Wolfville. In the most revealing of his many *Cosmopolitan* articles, "What Life Means to Me" (XLII, January 1907), Lewis, "with great frankness and sincerity," advances his theory of man's captivity in a hostile universal machine, a point of view often re-affirmed in Wolfville's psychological and spiritual environment. "Immersed in the world," Alfred Henry Lewis pries "among its wheels and cogs for motives," but concludes that "Civilization is an artifice, a trap, a deceit"; that man is necessarily a "fatalist," for "the future is decreed [while] he is locked helpless as the fly in amber"; and that "The weaker life that must be helped might better perish and make room for a stronger, more perfect life that can fend for itself." Ultimately, life can be reduced to this definition: "It means that the physical rules, and savagery sits on a hill. It means the omnipotence of chance. . . ."

Despite the immutable determinism he sees governing mankind, and despite the oppressive Social Darwinism underlying every principle of existence, Lewis avoids tumbling into the abyss of Mark Twain's Great Dark. Instead he positively asserts: "I am not mad with any ardor of pessimism . . . nor has my hope been seized of dyspepsia." His Old Cattleman, the worldly sage and custodian of Wolfville's values, aptly and directly states the homely prairie wisdom inherent in his way of life: "Life is like a dance hall; an' we'll nacherly keep on dancin' an' dyin' ontil the floor manager—whoever he is an' wherever he is—orders on the last walse, an' winds up the *baile* with the final call, 'All prom'nade to the bar of eternal jestice!' " ("The Jest of Talky Jones," *Wolfville Folks*, p. 213). Holding such a philosophic overview, The Old Cattleman represents the character, personality, and temper of his community, "cold sober," "joobilant," and "straight."

At the outset two sharply defined vignettes of Wolfville life serve to illustrate the emotional and psychological ambience of Lewis's frontier town. A reckless cowboy named Cottonwood

Wasson has sportively shot up a peaceful Oriental who was walking on his way to merchant Armstrong's store "to spend money." Having lost a prospective customer, the enraged storekeeper protests this uncalled-for intrusion into Wolfville's free enterprise system, a view supported that afternoon by philosophical gamblers at the faro table: "This Chinaman is out to buy soap or starch or blooin' or what other chem'cals he employs in his suds-sloppin'. . . . A Chinaman is one thing; but commerce must not an' shall not be shot up. . . . Wolfville will not tolerate interference with business interests. Yereafter, when moved to go burnin' up the scenery about a Chinaman with your gun, be shore it's after he makes his purchases" ("Cottonwood Wasson," *Wolfville Folks*, p. 173). The "Chinks," "opium slaves" and "heathens from the Orient," are wily Mongols sending the fear of Yellow Peril through the righteous community. Shooting them is, if not sport, at least civic duty; yet one must never act in restraint of trade. But while Chinese represent the satanic element of local society, conversely, the angelic is symbolized by the purifying, spiritually uplifting presence of white American women: "it's no sorter doubt they's the noblest an' most exhilaratin' work of their Redeemer" (*Wolfville*, p. 166). Absolute good and absolute evil, then, are quickly and vividly established in the Wolfville ethos.

Also markedly contributing to a clear picture of Lewis's Western town is the bizarre case of the man from Red Dog, a rival camp rowdy who shoots his way into Wolfville, assaults a Mexican couple, and threatens to "distribute this yere hamlet 'round in the landscape." He issues a challenge to the manhood of Wolfville: "I find you-alls is a lawless, onregenerate set, a heap sight worse than roomer. I now takes the notion—for I see no other trail—that by next drink time I climbs into the saddle, throws my rope 'round this den of sin, an' removes it from the map" ("The Man From Red Dog," *Wolfville*, p. 102). Boasting in the rhetoric of a nineteenth-century riverboatman, he

18

spews words over the attentive locals: "I drinks with friend, an' I drinks with foe; with the pard of my bosom an' the shudderin' victim of my wrath all sim'lar" (p. 103). Such verbal intimidation and inappropriate behavior—though well formulated by dime novel Western villains—cannot be tolerated, and before the episode draws to a close, the bragging interloper is cold-decked by Faro Nell, who has tampered with his gunsight. Then he is scalped by Cherokee Hall and killed amidst a circus of violence: "About the fifth fire the Red Dog man sorter steps for'ard an' drops his gun; an' after standin' onsteady for a second, he starts to cripplin' down at his knees. At last he comes ahead on his face like a landslide. Thar's two bullets plumb through his lungs, an' when we gets to him the red froth is comin' outen his mouth some plenteous" (p. 106).

The gunfight and all the events leading up to it illuminate the standard etiquette of Wolfville as well as the quality of life which the community tacitly condones. Basic assumptions underlying the everyday social dynamics of Wolfville, therefore, would read this way: Anglo-Saxon womanhood is deified; she is alone at the top of the great chain, whether she is washerwoman, bar girl, homemaker, or dancer. The white, Anglo-Saxon male of Wolfville who properly exercises "American jedgement" is next in order on the social hierarchy. In addition —since Western ancestral and cultural background is necessary for preservation of principles that are implied in *American jedgement*—Eastern dudes, who are objects of ridicule and persecution, as well as any other unfortunate outlanders or downright foreigners passing through the community, must be regarded with suspicion. Wolfville's citizens, furthermore, subscribed energetically to the same philosophy of law and order: "Let any outfit take a bale of rope an' a week off, an' if their camp ain't weeded down to right principles an' a quiet life at the end tharof, then I've passed my days as vain as any coyote which ever yelps" (*Wolfville*, p. 118). At the bottom of the

19

Wolfville social scale obviously are the Orientals, the Mexicans, and the Indians. Ugliest strangers were suspect only until they proved their "jedgement." But the minorities were never worth even this much consideration.

While the structure of this Arizona town suggests the chaos, even the anarchy, of a newly-exploding community that is reeling amidst its volatile social mixture, there are a few basic laws which are simple but nevertheless specific. In Wolfville, a cowboy cannot insult a woman, shoot his pistol in a place of business, ride his horse into a bar or store, or even deliberately ride onto the town's sidewalks. Transgressions of this nature are interpreted as direct challenges to the authority of the sheriff, who can watch the citizens—representing a cross section of a typical nineteenth-century Western town—while he is sauntering down the single street of Wolfville. These people are a transient assortment of transplanted Confederates and Castillians, ex-soldiers and mesquite diggers, Injuns and sheepherders, Eastern tourists and prairie dogs. Built to occupy the time and to fulfill the needs of these citizens are the Bird Cage Opera House, which is the center of serious entertainment, and the Red Light Saloon, where a patron can purchase Old Jordan, Valley Tan, Willow Run, and other "lickers which has a distinct tendency to make a gent sedate, an' render him plumb cer-monious so that he might even address a measly Mexican as Sir!" The New York Store is the local market for general supplies, while the O.K. House is Wolfville's hotel-restaurant, run under the shrewd, watchful eye of Mrs. Rucker, who simultaneously manages the enterprise, lectures her husband, and feeds the town's bachelors. Nearby, the Mexican *baile* hall, owned by Santa Rosa and his wife Marie, supplies "greaser" entertainment for the adventurous and the daring.

Certain key people appear and reappear in the Old Cattleman's narratives: Doc Peets, a medical man and "the wisest sharp in Arizona"; Cherokee Hall, a quiet card dealer who loves the beautiful "yearling," Faro Nell; Jack Moore, a man who is the executive officer of the vigilante organization known as the "Stranglers," and also a man whose cold-blooded nerve allows him to transact even fireworks "with a ca'm, offishul front"; Dave Tutt, dignified and lofty, and—as the husband of Tucson Jennie—one of the few married men in Wolfville; old Sam Enright, who is venerated for his wisdom, and who has "a mighty piercin' eye . . . [with] a gray gleam in it like the shine of a new bowie." This permanent cast of Wolfville's stable citizenry is rounded out by Dan Boggs, who has the "muscles of a cinnamon b'ar," by Texas Thompson, whose wife back in Laredo is—to Thompson's annoyance—agitating for a divorce, and by Old Monte, the whip-cracking Wells Fargo stage driver, who fears nothing from the dangers of road agents "as long as they don't interfere with the licker traffic."

Lewis portrays cultural disadvantages of Wolfville with kind, satiric humor. The nearest approach to literary aspiration in town is a "cirk'latin" library whose reprint copy of *Robinson Crusoe,* left by Texas Thompson on a chair outside the Red Light, is promptly eaten by a curious burro ("Long Ago on the Rio Grande," *Wolfville Nights,* p. 306). Indeed, the simple, sentimental side of the town's life is symbolized by this tombstone message from "Wolfville's First Funeral" (*Wolfville,* p. 8) :

LIfE AiN'T

in

HOLDING A GOOD HAND

but

IN PLAYING A PORE HAND

WELL

Occasionally a "dramy" will come to town at the Op'ry House, but during most late afternoons and evenings the men of Wolfville will gather at the Saloon to drink, to exchange tales, and to gossip "about cattle an' killin's, an' other topics common to a cow country." Here the past and present converge. The dreamy romance of Mexico and its era of grandees and the picturesque cultures of the Indian of antiquity mix with the cowboy culture of the New West with its primitive, simplistic, Darwinist philosophy of struggle for existence and survival of the fittest. For all its sense of nostalgia and romance, the ethic of Wolfville is predatory and violent. With such elemental and brutal struggle Lewis pictured the Western mystique in this attractive, "uncivilized" environment which he updated from the sensational Dime Novel days.

Alfred Henry Lewis's panorama of Wolfville, then, leaped from his creative imagination full blown, without an evolutionary process during which the community and its people moved toward new awareness or altered lifestyles to meet changing conditions. Tales in the volume *Wolfville* (1897), his first collection, and the tales in *Faro Nell and Her Friends* (1913), his last collection, are indistinguishable in content, idea, strategy, or style. The best illumination of the Lewis ethic and aesthetic, therefore, comes from an examination of those crucial themes which run through his Western fiction with significant repetition: religion, love, and integrity. To reflect these concepts Lewis, through the rugged and eloquent talespinning of his Old Cattleman, transcends the nineteenth-century Dime-Novel clichés to depict for popular audiences the Western community immersed in its daily dilemmas.

There is a humorous side to the religious experiences of Wolfville, and the fickle nature of some local worshippers is described by Tom, a black, who in the course of his lifetime has sampled many orthodoxies available in the town's churches. Feeling that the Presbyterian Church is "too gloomy," he then tries the Methodists:

> Thar's a deal mo' sunshine among d' Mefodis' folks, an' d' game's a mighty sight easier. All you does is get

sprunkled, an' thar you be, in wid d'sheep, kerzip! The objections I had to d' Mefodis' is them 'sperience meetin's they holds. They 'spects you to stan' up an' tell 'em about all yo' sins, an' fess all you've been guilty of endoorin' yo' life! . . . I'm too modes' to be a Mefodis'. So I . . . shins . . . out for d' Baptis' folks. . . . I'm at peace now: I'm in d' Baptis' chu'ch, sah. You go inter d' watah, kersause! an' that sets yo' safe in d' love of d' lamb. ("When the Stage Was Stopped," *Wolfville Days*, p. 296)

Despite Tom's strong endorsement, though, all is not love and peace in the Baptist fold:

They splits on doctrine . . . [so] you couldn't get 'em together with a gun. They disagree on Adam. That outfit in the valley holds that Adam was all right when he started, but later he struck something an' glanced off; them up on the hill contends that Adam was a hoss-thief from the jump. An' thar you be! You couldn't reeconcile 'em between now an' the crack of doom. Doctrines to a Baptis' that a-way is the entire checkrack. ("Death and the Donna Anna," *Wolfville Days*, p. 188)

For the most part, the role of religion was serious and significant. Rationalism, however, was the major orientation, although the town's enlightenment was curiously mixed with romance, even mystery.

"This yere West you hails from is roode, an' don't yield none to religious inflooences," a young preacher once confided to the Old Cattleman ("Slim Jim's Sister," *Wolfville*, p. 183); yet the divine has made a serious miscalculation, and he is thus cautioned: "But if you figgers we don't make our own little religious breaks out in Arizona, stranger, you figgers a heap wrong." The religion that Lewis's Cattleman tries to explain, then, is obviously at variance with the organized theological orthodoxy symbolized by traditional worship in the sophisticated United States. Energetic circuit riders, though, can hardly be silenced. They argue that the West needs churches like those in the East, in order to influence a "perverse generation" to abandon their "evil-doin'" (pp. 184-85). The undisciplined, seemingly chaotic pattern of life in Wolfville, indeed, led many a "gospel spreader" to "pitch camp" inside city limits to exhort "these yere onforchoonate mavericks, condemned as they be at birth to go pirootin' from the cradle to the grave" cursed by a "predom'natin' element of evil" ("The Funeral of Old Holt," *Faro Nell and Her Friends*, p. 297). It is not, however, the simple "old time" religion that hovers like a wary angel above tempestuous Wolfville. There are complications.

In a candid moment the Old Cattleman admits, "Well, I ain't shorely livin' in what you'd call 'grace,' still I has my beliefs." He elaborates pointedly: "Back in Tennessee my folks is Methodis', held to sprinklin' an' sech; however, for myse'f, I never banks none on them technicalities. It's deeds that counts with Omnipotence, same as with a vig'lance committee; an' whether a gent is sprinkled or dipped or is . . . averse to water . . . won't settle whether he wins out a harp or a hot pitchfork in the eternal beyond" ("The Defiance of Gene Watkins," *Wolfville Days*, p. 215). In this way the Cattleman has underscored a basic principle behind the spirit of the place. Rival camp Red Dog has been "out-lucked, out-dealt, out-held an' outplayed" because Wolfville has sought sanctification by works. Yet the community yearns toward even a higher spirituality: "What the hour pines for is the ameeloratin' an' mollifyin' inflooence of an elevated womanhood" ("Doc Peets' Error," *Wolfville Folks*, p. 99).

The ethos of womanhood, an essence of purity in the dessicated land of rolling tumbleweed, is another practical manifes-

24

tation of the Wolfville religious orientation. "Inflooence" is the prime requisite, and womanhood represents humanity's highest promise of good. In town, Faro Nell, Tucson Jennie, and Wagon Mound Sal are symbolic evangelists whose silent presence directs man's angelic instincts to seek holy perspectives. The mere visibility of these women arouses feelings of piety and awe, even in the most reprobate of sinners.

Of special consequence in the spirituality of Wolfville, too, is the prayer meeting that is generally organized by earnest travelling ministers who are sometimes intimidated by the brilliant candle light of the New York Store's warehouse and by an unruly congregation seated on improvised benches. When called upon to officiate at one such religious get-together, Old Man Enright appears to echo the sentiments of his friend the Cattleman: "This yere is a relig'ous meetin'. I am not myse'f given that a-way, but I'm allers glad to meet up with folks who be, an' see that they have a chance in for their ante, an' their game is preserved. I'm one, too, who believes a little religion wouldn't hurt this yere camp much. Next to a lynchin', I don't know of a more excellent inflooence in a western camp than these meetin's" ("Short Creek Dave," *Sandburrs*, p. 72). Salvation is always a nervous consideration, but the traditional "Gospel-gents" characteristically make little headway among the Wolfville individualists, though even Boggs came "mighty near bein' caught in some speritual round-up one time." Remaining true to himself, though, Boggs, resigned to damnation, escapes. "Thar's no good tryin' to hold out kyards on your Redeemer," he says. "If your heart ain't right it's no use to set into the game. No cold deck goes. He sees plumb through every kyard you holds, an' nothin' but a straight deal does with Him" ("Boggs's Experience," *Wolfville*, p. 218).

Wolfville people are fiercely superstitious souls, despite their reliance on simple fate and clear-headed rationalism. Devout believers in the spirit world, they are quick to assert great faith in artifacts, messages, and other psychic communications from the great beyond. Solemn in pointing out the naturally super-stitious attitudes of the benighted Indians and Mexicans, local citizens nonetheless look to occult emblems for explanations of man's actions and existence. One time, having won a pair of mules that had belonged to the estates of "some Mexican," the Cattleman finds "a cross marked on each harness an' likewise on both wagons." He thereupon explains:

> Mexicans employs this formal'ty to run a bluff on any evil sperit who may come projectin' round. Your Amer-ican mule skinner never makes them tokens. As a roole he's defiant of sperits; an' even when he ain't he don't see no refooge in a cross. Mexicans, on the other hand, is plenty strong on said symbol. Every mornin' you be-holds a Mexican with a dab of white on his fore'erd an' each cheek bone, an' also on his chin where he crosses himse'f with flour; shore, the custom is yooni-versal an' it takes a quart of flour to fully fortify a full-blown Greaser household ag'inst the antic'pated perils of the day." ("Tom and Jerry: Wheelers," *Wolfville Nights,* p. 129)

When a mesmerist comes to town "to give a exhibition of ana-mile magnetism [as well as to] cure what halt an' blind . . . is cripplin' an' moonin' about," enthusiastic townsfolk turn out fully expecting to witness the miracle ("Propriety Pratt, Hyp-notist," *Faro Nell,* p. 192). They are disappointed; but their faith is not disturbed.

A belief in the prophecy of "kyards" is also held with sacred fervor in Wolfville. The "hand the dead man held" is a clear, frightful foreboding that "Death is fixin' his sights" on some random unfortunate marked for the grave ("Jacks upon Eights," *Wolfville,* p. 156). Dan Boggs emphatically articulates his personal belief in spectres that perform acts of dark vengeance, like those fearful ghosts that can stampede a host of cow punchers ("The Ghost of the Bar - B-8," *Wolfville Nights,* p. 162). With aplomb, even the respected Colonel Sterett expresses his belief that the supernatural has populated the moon itself! "The face of that orb is simply festered with folks! She teems with life; ant-hills on election day means desertion by compar'son. Thar's thousands an' thousands of people, mobbin' about indiscrim'nate; I sees 'em . . . ." ("Colonel Sterett Relates Marvels," *Wolfville Nights,* p. 268). Even though the citizens of Lewis's town are intimidated by the unknown, though they simultaneously fear, respect, and insult Bible-thumpers, though omens and psychic admonitions scorch their frontier sensibilities with the heat of a prairie fire, they remain quietly resigned to the basic common-sense philosophy of religion as a kind of fatalism. "Myst'ry—all myst'ry!" asserts the Old Cattleman; "the more a gent goes messin' for s'lootions, the more he's taught hoomility an' that he ain't knee-high to toads" ("How the Mocking Bird Was Won," *Faro Nell,* p. 126).

In his essay "What Life Means to Me," Lewis emphasizes this viewpoint, however ambiguous or naive it may seem. In the long run, this belief permeates the spiritual orientation of his Wolfville crowd: "Life is a mystery and I cannot solve it. I sit at the window of existence and look out on the world. I ask myself those questions which men have ever asked themselves . . . . The future? It is a bridge I shall cross when I come to it" (p. 293). He looks with resignation toward a possible confrontation with another world: "Ever I am face to face with paradox—the paradox of time, the paradox of space. I understand and don't understand, know and don't know. I look into the heavens' fenceless depths, and know they can have no end, no frontier, no beyond. Also I am incapable of the endless. The same with time. It is as though my intelligence had received a blow in the face. Feeling myself finite I draw back from the infinite . . . . The certain diminishes, while the uncertain expands. . . ." (p. 293). Evading fundamental questions concerning theology and belief, Lewis portrayed his Wolfville people as having a childlike adherence to the formalities and formulas of conventional worship. Moreover, they have a respect—born of fright—for all unrevealed psychic and spiritualistic phenomena. What current science cannot readily explain to them, they consider a mystical truth. Thereupon they propound these mystical truths in local barrooms and whisper them in fireside tales. Not even "a progressif an' enlightened" newspaper that is devoted to the "mental and material upheaval" of the "commoonity" dares to challenge revelations that are sent from some great beyond! ("The Wolfville Daily Coyote," *Wolfville Days,* p. 64).

Love, soft and sentimental, prevails despite the otherwise abrasive and harsh elements of Wolfville. "I'm actooally hungerin' for a love story," sharp-talking Faro Nell confesses to "Daddy" Enright, who is about to spin a sad tale of romance and war, a tale about a light-hearted soldier and a Mexican beauty of eighteen. Occasionally the rosy aura of love and sentiment colors everything in the camp of Wolfville. Sex symbols like Faro Nell, Tucson Jennie, and Wagon Mound Sal discover abject reverence in the lovelorn hearts that inhabit an otherwise brutal, careless town where the crude, hostile by-laws of a Darwinist universe are the only statutes. The presence of these women, however, eventually creates a variety of religious exhilaration foreign to Western settlements that have been deprived of the feminine mystique. The presence of women also instills in the Wolfville men the spirit of romantic love and its higher inspiration. So, while farobank, monte, and roulette hold "prosperous sway" as a man's pastime, an even greater and more interesting diversion is the quadrille at the dance hall. The dance is accompanied by a verse "carrollin'" the loveliness of Wolfville femininity ("When Tutt First Saw Tucson," *Wolfville Nights,* p. 208):

Fair as a lily bloomin' in May,
Sweeter than roses, bright as the day!
Everyone who knows her feels her gentle power
Rosalie the Prairie Flower.

Yet wherever in Wolfville the serene passion prevails, the recurring motifs are those of love mocked by comedy and of love saddened by unalterable social conditions or thwarted by unexpected events.

A prototype of the love heroine is Polly Hawks, who nurses Sam Enright back to health after the good man has tangled with a bear: "Polly is big an' strong . . . her eyes is like stars, an' she's as full of sweetness as a bee tree or a bar'l of m'lasses. So Polly camps down by my couch of pain an' begins dallyin' soothin'ly with my heated brow . . . . Polly . . . [is] an alloorin' form of hooman hollyhock . . . [she is] as sweet an' luscious as a roast apple." One of this damsel's suitors is the "blood-drinkin' skelp-t'arin, knife-plyin' demon of Sunflower Creek" who courts his lady love in "blanket verse": "Polly Hawks shall marry an' follow me to my wigwam! Her bed shall be of b'ar-skins; her food shall be yearlin' venison, an' wild honey from the tree! Her gown shall be panther's pelts fringed 'round with wolf-tails an' eagles' claws! She shall belt herself with a rattle-snake, an' her Sunday bonnet shall be a swarm of bees! . . . We will wed an' pop'late the earth with terror! Where is the sooi-cide who'll stand in my way" ("Old Man Enright's Love," *Wolfville Days,* pp. 274-75). Fate intervenes, however, and now Enright—like so many of his peers in the town—has only romantic memories of this brief nostalgic interlude. Love in Wolfville often drives even the most sensible souls to inexplicable excess.

One adventure in particular involves a phenomenon that is new on the American scene, a "specific heroine . . . a heap on-conventional" who is an early version of the Feminist incendiary, a "Twentieth-Century New Woman" looking to assert her independence. Wolfville, as one might reasonably expect, is scarcely ready for her. "I'm a se'f-respectin', se'f-supportin' young female, who believes in Woman Suffrage, an' the equality of the sexes in pol'tics an property rights," she asserts. Her name is Cythiana Bark, and she has been nicknamed Original Sin. Her purpose is "to become a citizen of this yere camp, an' take my ontrammeled place in its commercial life by openin' a grogshop" ("Cythiana, Pet-named Original Sin," *Faro Nell,* p. 69). Her eyes are "as soft as the sky in Joone" but, however coquettishly, she flourishes a mean-looking Winchester whose trigger she is not afraid to squeeze. Understanding this different species of female is impossible for Wolfville. The bewildered Boggs, wondering whether there are many of this breed, is informed by the learned Peets that "The Eastern ranges is alive with 'em. But they don't last. As a roole they gets married, an' that's gen'rally speakin' the end of their pernicious activ'ties" (p. 72).

Even the Wolfville women unanimously reject the revolutionary views propounded by this aggressive, strange young lady. "Missis" Rucker expresses the prevailing sentiment: "She's welcome . . . to her feelin's; but she mustn't come preachin' no doctrine to me, wharof the effects is to lower me to Rucker's level" (p. 73). At times Faro Nell herself appears to be an emancipated female; yet she never stoops to endorse such radicalism. Original Sin, however, is out to politicize Wolfville, hoping to make women the proprietors of all the saloons. Once feminists control the "nosepaint" of the nation, she believes, "the ballot is bound to follow."

In some ways, Cythiana Bark, though isolated by her aggressive feminist stance, fits well into Wolfville society. One week after her stormy arrival into the town, she kills her first "Greaser" because he was "roode." She shoots a fusillade of bullets at an Eastern dude merely to "skeer" him. And though

30

she preaches Woman Suffrage "incessant," her proselytizing never interferes with the efficient pursuit of her money-making business. Predictably Cythiana captures a bridegroom, a slender, effete "shorthorn," and gives up her crusade in Wolfville so that she can live in a proper home back East. Despite her bravado, domesticity was what she really desired. Lewis tells a tale of Western excitement but manages to preserve the conventions of romantic fiction that were so popular among young American girls.

Love and romance frequently blossom among the most unlikely people of the town. Riley Bent is a happily confirmed bachelor, and Sal is the mistress of a laundry. They meet while she is sudsing—for the second time—a tub of blue woollen shirts. Instantly, Sal falls into love of such depth that this resolute young lady decides to take unsuspecting Riley Bent for better or for worse. She silently stalks her game, but Bent philosophizes that marriage is "onnacheral." A shoot-out, a sheriff's pistol, and a threat of the Stranglers, however, make the heart of Riley Bent "romantic an' sentimental." Suddenly, under these intimidating circumstances, his mind is softened to "lead that lady to the altar" ("Wagon Mound Sal," *Sandburrs,* pp. 143, 151).

The principal conventions of love in Wolfville, however, are merely formal courtship, traditional marriage with a "gospel-sharp" presiding, and an orthodox home life with the usual responsibilities. Sentiments in the camp are against "a married female takin' in washin'." According to wise Doc Peets, "What we wants is the picture of a happy household where the feminine part tharof, in the triple capacity of woman, wife an' mother, while cherishin' an' carin' for her husband, sheds likewise a radiant inflooence for us" ("Mistress Killifer," *Sandburrs,* p. 215).

Household skirmishes and explosions sometimes occur even among these reasonable folks. "Missis Rucker goes on surroundin' old Rucker with connoobial joy to sech a degree that, one mornin' when her wifely back is turned, he ups an' stampedes off into the hills, an' takes refutch with the Apaches" ("The Widow Dangerous," *Wolfville Folks*, p. 1). Still, husbands like old Rucker always return, for stability is the essential characteristic of the Wolfville marriage. Even so, through all the Wolfville tales there is a running joke about the plight of Texas Thompson, who is apparently headed for divorce and is worried about having to pay alimony. Reasons for the break-up are unclear, but fear and inertia keep him from joining his estranged, temperamental spouse in Laredo.

In a highly publicized union, Dave Tutt and Tucson Jennie become the married couple which Wolfville most pridefully adopts. But even though this loving pair had originally "tumbled into housekeepin' peaceful as two pups in a basket," ("Tucson Jennie's Jealousy," *Wolfville*, p. 80), their marriage has to survive some bumpy trails. A misunderstanding over an English "towerist" drives Jennie from her home and family, and she goes back to the kitchen of the O.K. House for her old job. Enraged, she deserts the bemused Tutt, behaves "illogical" and "onresponsible," and drives her husband "plumb locoed" with frustration. Although Tutt is only an "amature husband," he wants to "round-up" and return his wife. Appealing to what he considers the universal feminine psychology—East or West —Tutt visits the New York Store to "win her out some duds," and when the angry Jennie "sees the raiment" her "heart melts" as she "ropes onto the dry goods an' starts sobbin' out for the 'doby where she an' Dave lives at" (p. 95).

The crisis is past. Whether washerwoman or bar girl, the Alfred Henry Lewis woman of the West is no different from the Lady of the Decoration, whose presence was so characteristic in most drawing-room sentimental fiction of the era before World War I. Even Faro Nell, a prairie-hardened woman, is given to romantic dreaming "like all girls, full of fancies that a-way" ("How Tutt Shot Texas Thompson," *Faro Nell*, p. 281).

Perhaps the best Wolfville story is the Old Cattleman's romantic tale in *Wolfville Days* of "Death and the Donna Anna," in which Lewis dramatizes the love ethic of this Western community in a mature and moving way, and where he avoids over-sentimentalizing. Here Lewis is able to dominate the materials of the story and—however stereotyped they initially appear to be—to mould his people into a statement which captures the real spirit of love in rowdy Wolfville. The tale dramatizes, too, the fact that ethnic animosities between *Mexicano* and *gringo* may be transcended by love.

Indirectly the story begins with a learned discussion of *oxytropis lamberti,* that is, of loco weed and its poisonously narcotic effects upon man and animal. From here the Cattleman moves to a discussion of mules, Injuns, and Mexicans as he lectures on "illoosions" and fantasies, intelligence and locoweed. From this point the storyteller moves easily into a tale of love, locoweed, and Mexico. The heroine of the Cattleman's yarn is Donna Anna, who, according to any "connoshur of female loveliness," is a genuine "miracle. She's as beautiful as a cactus flower; an' as vivid. She's tall an' strong . . . with a voice like velvet, graceful as a mountain lion, an' with eyes that's soft an' deep an' black, like a deer's. She's . . . as dark an' as warm an' as full of life as a night in Joone" (p. 192). Anna falls hopelessly in love with "Lootenant" Jack Spencer, a soldier of refined, genteel Southern family. But their passion must end in tragedy, for the mundane complications of life and the twists of fate bring inevitable sadness. The Old Cattleman repeats the agonized account that Donna Anna has given her priest:

> He came, the Senor Juan . . . and I gave him all my love. But in a day he was to have gone to his home far away with the Americanos. Then I would never more see him, nor hear him, and my soul would starve and die. There, too, was a Senorita, an Americana; she would have my place. Father [priest], what could I do?

I gave him the loco to drink; not much, but it was enough. Then his memory sank and sank; and he forgot the Senorita Americana; and he remembered not to go away to his home; and he became like a little child with me. The good loco drove every one from his heart; and all from his mind—all, save me, the Donna Anna. I was the earth and the life to him. And so, night and day, since he came until now he dies, my arms and my heart have been about the Senor Juan. (p. 201)

The loco has reduced Spencer to a *muchachito*, a child, and Anna becomes simultaneously his lover and mother. She knows also that "none may live who drinks the loco," and as her temporal happiness ends, she looks forward eagerly to being with him in the hereafter. She commits suicide on his grave. Her understanding padre observes that the pair will escape everlasting perdition, even though they have sinned, for "They were guiltless of all save love; and the good God does not punish love" (p. 202).

In an unsystematic but revealing manner, Lewis details, then, expressions of love in Wolfville. Women, he asserts through his Cattleman, ought to conform readily to the expectations and formalities of their place in the social fabric. They are to be protected, of course, even revered, for they represent the ethereal amidst the pedestrian. But they possess all the wiles to influence men as the women see fit. Females are more susceptible to the overwhelming power of love, and any deed in love's name can be effectively rationalized. Therefore, female duties and responsibilities include a high degree of domestic competence, ferocious family loyalty, and demonstrable physical courage. In fact, the more "maleness" may appear in the character and personality of the local ladies, the more likely it is that Wolfville femininity is inherent in their make-up. In addition to the household arts, the "good" woman should also be able to deal cards, tend bar, and ride and shoot well enough to retrieve an errant, wandering spouse. Though in these respects Lewis has paid his occasional dues to romantic fiction—his caricatures resemble Bret Harte's—he has successfully avoided the obviously mawkish scenes of "hearts and flowers" which the flood of western hacks disgorged in paperback Dime Novels of the period.

Integrity governs all behavior and motivation in the frontier community that Alfred Henry Lewis has created. What Zane Grey was later to label the "Code of the West" controls the morality and the ethics of Wolfville. Here, American patriotism, a need for swift, retributive justice, and an essential belief in courage, fair play, and honor all watch like philosophic gods over the sagebrush and tumbleweed. Frequently Lewis contrasts the rugged democracy of the West with the waning culture of the decadent East. He contrasts, too, the Western Man with the Eastern tenderfoot and shows that the Wolfville citizen is the better of the two. He describes again and again the veneration of infants and "old timers" that prevails among the people of the prairie; and through repeated expressions of White Supremacy that reflect virulent prejudices against Chinese, Indians, and Mexicans, Lewis reveals the strong racism that prevailed in the camps of the West ("Piñon Bill's Bluff," *Wolfville*, pp. 310-325; "With the Apache's Compliments," *Wolfville Nights*, pp. 99-108) . This life is an elemental one, and the society is simplistic, but the human relationships, the codes of behavior, are official and formal. This qualitative integrity ultimately stabilizes the Old Cattleman's town. More than religion and more than love, integrity is the trait by which Wolfville and its folk must ultimately be assessed.

The basic tenets of Wolfville's integrity require that a person must live and die by a code sometimes ratified in blood and always accepted with the confidence that a Fundamentalist would have in a Biblical text. Protocols of address, rules that govern card games and horse thieves, and regulations that have to do with appropriate behavior on the streets of town are basic cowboy facts. But total integrity requires the understanding that virtually every activity in Wolfville is orchestrated and ritualized. Even highway bandits have a guide book which they are supposed to follow:

> Thar's rooles about stage robbin', same as thar is to faro-bank an' poker. It's onderstood by all who's interested, from the manager of the stage company to the gent in the mask who's holdin' the Winchester on the outfit, that the driver don't fight. He's thar to drive, not shoot; an' so when he hears the su'gestion, 'Hands up!' that a-way, he stops the team, sets the brake, hooks his fingers together over his head, an' nacherally lets them road agents an' passengers an' gyards, settle events in their own onfettered way. The driver, usual, cusses out the brigands frightful. The laws of the trail accords him them privileges, imposin' no reestrictions on his mouth. He's plumb free to make what insultin' observations he will, so long as he keeps his hands up an' don't start the team none ontil he's given the proper word; the same comin' from the hold-ups or the gyards, whoever emerges winner from said emeutes [riots]. ("When the Stage Was Stopped," *Wolfville Days*, p. 299)

As a result, the real and the ideal stage robbery become the same in the Wolfville ethos, for the parts are played by formula, with any improvisation likely to be catastrophic. The individual who wantonly transgresses the rules, furthermore, must expect just punishment, for the unwritten law of the town remains the only stability in this frontier society.

There are ways, sometimes cruel but always effective and

socially acceptable, by which the community deals with those who accidentally or deliberately break these tacitly accepted rules. Toothpick Johnson, for example, "disgraced" Wolfville by downing "a party an' no gun on the gent." Here, perhaps, is the most flagrant sin one can commit: killing an unarmed man. Events at a card table have led to the shooting, and while no one blames Toothpick, who has mistakenly thought that his adversary was reaching for a gun, "the public sort o' longs for his eelopement" ("Toothpick Johnson's Ostracism," *Wolfville Days*, p. 57). Toothpick's problem is that he is "too simooltaneous"; so "no one talks of stringin' him for what's a plain case of bad jedgment, an' nothin' more." It remains for Old Man Enright to pronounce Wolfville's sentence on the man who cannot hold his six-shooter in "abeyance," a man who is "a heap too soon." Even though the people of Wolfville "exonerates" the accused man, Enright suggests, in the pointed vernacular of the time, that if anybody came looking for Toothpick at sundown the next day and found him still in Wolfville, they would "hang you some" (p. 62). The integrity of the community is at stake. Its reputation for fair play and justice must be preserved. Toothpick must go.

The Wolfville Code functions alike for upright citizen and for outlaw. Deviation is unacceptable, the most vivid case in point being Silver City Philip, who quickly becomes anathema to the community. He is more than an outlaw; he is a "degen'rate," with all the marks of the deviate. He does not have the physique of an acknowledged highwayman. He is "a little, dark, ignorant, tousled-ha'red party . . . black an' small an' evil-seemin' as a Mexican." Even worse, he "has a quick, hyster'cal way like a woman or a bird." He is "allers like a cat; savage, gore-thirsty, yet shy, prideless, an' ready to fly." Once imprisoned, he escapes by taking a hostage, and with "his moral nacher onbalanced congenital," he plans to murder Faro Nell. Because Phil is capable of such "anamile" behavior, he cannot be dignified with a Code outlaw's death at the hands of the Stranglers or in common gun play. Seizing this "scrap of a man" who has stopped to load his six-shooter, Dan Boggs dashes Phil "ag'inst the flint-hard earth . . . till Silver Phil is nothin' but shattered bones an' bleedin' pulp" ("The Dismissal of Silver Phil," *Wolfville Nights*, p. 37). The integrity of the community remains untainted.

This violent sense of honor and integrity contributes to the unmourned passing of Curly Ben, who is a "most ornery" hard case, "a rustler of cattle, an' a smuggler of Mexican goods." Hired by Captain Moon to shoot an especially bloodthirsty Indian agent, Ben returns to Wolfville to do some private bargaining with his employer. "Jest as I onlimbers my six-shooter to get him where he lives, he offers me five thousand dollars to come back yere an' kill you," says Curly Ben to Captain Moon. "The question now is, do you raise this yere gent?" ("The Treachery of Curly Ben," *Wolfville Days*, pp. 105-06). Agreeing to raise the ante—though he never intends to enter this obscene bidding—Moon leaves, only to return a few minutes later to shoot Ben dead with a bullet through the back of his skull. As a formality, Wolfville's committee of vigilance brings the killer to trial. But these Kangaroo Court judges "throws Moon loose," basing their acquittal on a fiction that Curly Ben one time back East had "delooded" Moon's sister and that now the "base sedoocer" has been justly punished by an understandable irate brother. In Wolfville, treachery is intolerable. It is even more intolerable when it is motivated by avarice.

In Wolfville, Fate governs the lives of the people, and it causes each person to behave properly according to the Code of Integrity. Without tears and without recrimination one must accept the future. As Cherokee Hall sees the scheme of things in Wolfville, "Life is like stud-poker; an' Destiny's got an ace buried every time . . . you can't bluff Destiny. All you-all can do is humbly . . . pick up the five kyards that belongs to you, an' in a sperit of thankfulness an' praise, an' frankly admittin' that you're lucky to be allowed to play at all, do your lowly best tharwith" ("The Defiance of Gene Watkins," *Wolfville Days*, p. 224).

Though Destiny places limits upon the exercise of free will, there are times in Wolfville when unorthodox occurrences require some flexibility of the rules by which men live and die. At such times, the harsh reality of the Code comes into direct conflict with a strain of romanticism.

Horse stealing is an intolerable crime. Patiently, the Old Cattleman explains why: "Son . . . if you was to put in three months in a cactus desert, with water holes fifty miles apart, it would begin to glimmer on you as to what it means to find yourse'f afoot. It would come over you like a landslide that the party who steals your hoss would have improved your condition in life a heap if he'd played his hand out by shootin' a hole through your heart" ("How the Dumb Man Rode," *Wolfville Days*, p. 136). There is unanimous agreement that "thar ain't only one side to hoss-stealin', an' the sooner the party's strung up or plugged, the sooner thar's a vict'ry for the right." On one occasion, however, a horse thief is deaf and dumb. Frustrated and bewildered, the local vigilantes try to communicate with the man, who desperately "puts up a few bluffs with his fingers." Pity for the dumb man leads to nervous hesitation. A note is discovered in the miscreant's pocket: "Dear Ben: Myra is dyin'; come at once. A." Now the men are overcome by what the Cattleman calls a "moral epidemic," whereupon they decide that "We can't afford to go makin' a preecedent of hangin' a gent for hoss-stealin' who's only doin' his best to be present at this Myra's fooneral" (p. 141).

On the day a notorious sot from the hated community of Red Dog—"Where the whiskey is speshul malignant"—dies in the Red Light Saloon, Wolfville's sympathetic instincts are quickly aroused when the deceased's dear old mother from Mis-

souri decides to attend the funeral. The reasoning of the Wolfville residents is that the lady has been "delooded" by her reprobate son into believing that he is one of the West's most illustrious citizens. Instead of the Boot Hill pauper's grave he really
deserves, the people of Wolfville bury Whiskey Billy with obse-
quies that are worthy of "the bravest, brightest gent in Arizona"
("When Whiskey Billy Died," *Wolfville Days*, p. 289). In such
cases as these, the chivalric code of Wolfville triumphs over the
Code of Integrity. On the other hand, when attorney Aaron
Green agrees to defend a handful of murderers, he finds that
the Stranglers have made "a house cleanin'." In the middle of
the street an astonished Aaron Green beholds "his entire docket
hangin' to the windmill" ("The Clients of Aaron Green," *Wolfville*, p. 262). The milk of human kindness in Wolfville is apparently selective, and sentiment is a haphazard virtue.

What Wolfville truly admires, though, is the dedication to
an ideal which defies even the possibility of death. The humorous tale of "Spelling Book Ben" illustrates the singular, even
fanatical sense of purpose that makes it unthinkable for a Wolfville man to deny his integrity as the "boss speller of the Rio
Grande." Ben is engaged to serve as "ringer" in a spelling bee
contest between Wolfville and Red Dog, his major opposition
being a Wells Fargo bookkeeper, who regards himself as "the
leadin' speller of eight States and two territories" ("Spelling
Book Ben," *Faro Nell*, p. 347). Sensing defeat, the "bookkeep"
jams his gun into Ben's ribs and demands that Ben spell "co-
lander" with a "u." Ben "never flickers" and begins "C-o-"
only to be shot dead by the frustrated Wells Fargo agent. Regarded as a valiant knight, Ben is given a hero's funeral and a
tombstone bearing this inscription (p. 322):

To
The Memory Of
Spelling Book Ben.
Preferring Death to The
Appearance of Ignorance
He Died
A Martyr To Learning And
Bravely
Defending A Rightful Orthography.
The Language Mourns
His Loss.

Spelling Book Ben's death does not exemplify a facile, slapstick suicide but a ratification of the Code in blood.

When he took pen in hand to write of politics, Alfred Henry Lewis candidly assessed the conditions of the times and expressed the philosophy that lay behind his writing of the Wolfville tales. Lewis's biography of Richard Croker, a notorious nineteenth-century Tammany Hall figure, deals with America's "moral stagnation" and excoriates the business ethic for instilling in otherwise honest and honorable people a set of mindless, corrosive values and some tortuous ethical rationalizations: "It is the age of avarice; of commercialism and a mania of money" (p. 317). It is "an age benumbed of commerce." Such a time has reduced man to the lowest level of basic passions: "Humanity . . . parts into a duo of classes, just as do animals; one being wild and the other domestic . . . the sheep people and the wolf people" (p. 324). While sanctimonious and smug Easterners revile the simplistic codes of justice, law, and order in Western communities, the legal system of the East, clothed in "vapid and mindless conventionality" (p. 198), has failed to bring order and security to the public there. From his study in New York, Alfred Henry Lewis turned West and wrote an impassioned defense of vigilante justice:

The first Americanism, and with it the first safety of life and limb, goods and good repute, are to be found in the South and West where your committee of vigilance can be convened at call. That committee is the best expression of the popular will. It comes up through no crookedness of tortuous and interested legislation; it smells of no vote-rottenness; it is as bribeless as a storm, as much beyond corruption as the light of day. It has but one thought: justice. And it never fails. One may say of committees of vigilance what one may not of courts. No committee of vigilance ever hanged the wrong man, nor let the wrong man go. (p. 199)

This excessive zeal, giving rise to opinions unsupported by documentation, clearly reveals the Lewis allegiances and loyalties. His Old Cattleman expresses similar opinions: "That's one of the excellent feachures about a vigilance committee, a feachure wharin they lays over other triboonals. All onbiased, they comes together before the witnesses grow lookewarm or the facts turn cold" ("The Heir of the Broken-O," *Wolfville Folks*, p. 119).

As America leaped into the twentieth century, and as in lurid headlines the journalism of the muckrakers exposed monopolistic greed, social exploitation, and political abomination, Lewis looked back upon the palmy days of his young manhood. There were fewer pressures then, and because men had been closer to nature, their emotions had been more honest and unsophisticated. In his reminiscences, Lewis would recall the "warm hearts," the "friendly fervor," the "marvelous serenity" of the "old faces" ("Confessions," *Human Life*, August 1906, p. 7). The backgrounds of "woolly Wolfville" had evolved as Lewis "sat cozily by a poker table" looking on with interest as an occasional toper would lapse into an amusing, entertaining imitation of Geronimo or some other prairie celebrity.

Negative influences were at work, too. Rapidly caught up in the passions of the Southwest, Lewis, unfortunately, developed animosities toward the resident Mexicans and editorialized in the Las Vegas *Optic*, "I reminded them that they were an inferior race, little if any better than the beasts that perish" (September 1906, p. 10). His vitriolic prejudice and his attraction to code and landscape fused in Lewis's creative intellect. The montage created by his Wolfville tales contained both the beauty of and the blemishes on the region. When long- and short-haul railroad economic wars were in progress, when everyday machinations in bucket-shops and manipulations in high finance were controlling human destinies with impersonal authority, Alfred Henry Lewis returned to the simple living in the West that had so dazzled and glamorized his younger days. Essentially, then, Wolfville constituted a world into which the artist escaped and through which he tried to understand early twentieth-century American civilization. The "O.K. Restauraw" was real; Delmonico's of New York was the illusion. The garrulous Cattleman of Alfred Henry Lewis caught that transient moment when the New West was striving for its identity, when the past and the future met on the mud-spattered boards of a cow town, and when the mechanical sounds of developing technology were starting to be heard close to Wolfville itself.

Alfred Henry Lewis also tried his hand at the Western story without Wolfville and the Old Cattleman. He indulged in a conventional novelist's picture of the West, and he dismally failed, most notoriously in *The Sunset Trail* (1905) and *The Throwback: A Romance of the Southwest* (1906). The former glorifies the exploits of Bat Masterson, the celebrated Dodge City hero, whose fictional gun play—specifically directed against Indians—eventually wins him the love of a beauty from Boston. This was fiction with "less fun and more gore," asserted the *Outlook* (May 20, 1905, p. 195), impatient with the thin plot and melodramatic action. *The Throwback*, too, is a disappointing tale. About an aristocrat turned buffalo hunter and sharp-shooter, the novel describes the former Eastern dude correctly and properly, perhaps, but without the color and intuition of the Cattleman: "[Robert Blainey] was sickly, melancholy, selfish, cruel without courage, full of book-cleverness, with a bent for plot and intrigue, and an innate preference for profit based on wrong. There was something repellent in his sallow skin, thin querulous lips, lank black hair, and small, dark complaining eyes" (p. 30). Rejuvenated by the West, this pathetic character soon becomes the scourge of the Panhandle. The New York *Times* noted that Lewis had "tamed his usual picturesque Wolfville language" (April 21, 1906, p. 254), and the *Critic* scathed this trivial effort for its "silliness" (August 1906, p. 191).

Alfred Henry Lewis had found his voice, and he never should have relinquished it. "We like these gentlemen of imaginative, figurative speech," states the *Independent* in reviewing *Wolfville Folks* (September 3, 1908, p. 550). The influential and prestigious *Nation* took careful note of Wolfville's literary stature and said of the Lewis Western synthesis, "Taking [Wolfville] dialect and story together . . . [they] tug at those muscles of mirth that Artemus Ward first played upon. One feels almost like an Englishman discovering American humor" (June 4, 1908, p. 516). Indeed, when Lewis learned—as had Emerson Hough—that the features of a cowboy's "daily surroundings and daily occupation . . . were intense, large, Homeric" (*The Story of a Cowboy*, p. 236), he had already appropriated for his literary system the essential overview that brought recognition and appreciation to the Old Cattleman and his community. With unassuming dignity and noble simplicity, Lewis brought to early twentieth-century readers a close-up vision of the Western ethos. In the Wolfville stories he examined that segment of the American Dream that was unfolding across the plains.

Selected Bibliography

Manuscript Material

There are ten letters of Alfred Henry Lewis to Albert Bigelow Paine in the Henry E. Huntington Library, San Marino, California.

Fiction by Alfred Henry Lewis

The Apaches of New York. New York: G. W. Dillingham, 1912.

The Black Lion Inn. New York: R. H. Russell, 1903.

The Boss and How He Came to Rule New York. New York: A. S. Barnes, 1903.

Confessions of a Detective. New York: A. S. Barnes, 1906.

Faro Nell and Her Friends: Wolfville Stories. New York: G. W. Dillingham, 1913.

Peggy O'Neal. Philadelphia: Drexel Biddle, 1903.

The President. New York: A. S. Barnes, 1904.

Sandburrs. New York: Frederick A. Stokes, 1900.

The Sunset Trail. New York: A. S. Barnes, 1905.

The Throwback: A Romance of the Southwest. New York: Outing, 1906.

Wolfville. New York: Frederick A. Stokes, 1897.

Wolfville Days. New York: Frederick A. Stokes, 1902.

Wolfville Folks. New York: D. Appleton, 1908.

Wolfville Nights. New York: Frederick A. Stokes, 1902.

Non-Fiction by Alfred Henry Lewis

A. Book

Richard Croker. New York: Life, 1901.

B. Articles

"Confessions of a Newspaperman." *Human Life* (November 1905-December 1906) : fourteen installments. A significant survey of turn-of-the-century American journalism, politics, urban life, and the West.

"Owners of America." *Cosmopolitan* (June, August-November, 1908) : five installments examining the careers of the following American "Captains of Industry": Andrew Carnegie, Thomas F. Ryan, J. Pierpont Morgan, Charles M. Schwab, and John D. Rockefeller.

"What Life Means to Me." *Cosmopolitan*, January 1907, 293-98. The "Lewis philosophy" which pervades all his fiction.

Secondary Sources

Filler, Louis. "Wolfville." *New Mexico Quarterly Review* (Spring 1943), 35-47.

Humphries, Rolfe. "Introduction." *Wolfville Yarns of Alfred Henry Lewis*. Kent, Ohio: The Kent State University Press, 1968. Pp. v-xviii.

There is virtually no considerable secondary source material on Lewis. A few sentences scattered throughout regional literary histories, a few paragraphs in standard American literature bibliographical texts, some basic data in the usual biographical reference works, and an occasional reference to the man and his writing in Western Americana surveys comprise the scholarship to date. These few brief references are listed in Richard W. Etulain's *Western American Literature: A Bibliography of Interpretive Books and Articles* (Vermillion: University of South Dakota Press, 1972), p. 87. The only bulk of commentary on Lewis—and not too considerable at that—is to be found in the contemporary reviews of his books.